# LIVING IN HARMONY

**LIVING IN HARMONY**
Sri Mata Amritanandamayi Devi

*Published by:*
  Mata Amritanandamayi Mission Trust
  Amritapuri PO, Kollam Dt., Kerala,
  INDIA 690 525
  Email: info@theammashop.org
  Website: www.amritapuri.org

Copyright © 2000 by Mata Amritanandamayi Mission Trust

All rights reserved. No part of this publication may be stored in a retrieval system, transmitted, reproduced, transcribed or translated into any language, in any form, by any means without the prior agreement and written permission of the publisher.

——— *Amma's UN Speech 2000 (English)* ———

February 2001 – June 2009: 16,000 copies
June 2012: 1000 copies

*Typesetting and Layout:* Amrita DTP, Amritapuri

# LIVING IN HARMONY

*An address given by*
Sri Mata Amritanandamayi Devi

*at the*
**Millennium World Peace Summit of
Religious and Spiritual Leaders**

The United Nations General Assembly
August 29, 2000

Mata Amritanandamayi Mission Trust
Amritapuri P.O., Kollam 690 525, Kerala, India

# Contents

| | |
|---|---|
| Foreword | 5 |
| Introduction | 9 |
| Living in Harmony | 19 |
|     The World is One Family | 23 |
|     Assimilating the Essence of Religions | 27 |
|     A New Age of Harmony Among Religions | 29 |
|     Recognising Areas of Conflict | 30 |
|     Cultivating Tolerance and Healing the Wounds of Conflict | 32 |
|     Freedom of Religion | 33 |
|     The Problem of Conversion | 33 |
|     Extremism | 34 |
|     Inner Transformation – The Key to Real Peace | 35 |
|     Spiritual Principles in Education | 36 |
|     Economic Inequality | 37 |
|     The Duty of Nations | 39 |
|     No Effort is Futile | 40 |

*Aum Amriteshwaryai Namah*

# Foreword

It was a very special get-together—three days of joy and renewed optimism, of sharing wisdom and experience, when religious leaders from over 150 countries gathered in the General Assembly hall at the United Nations Organisation. At a time when the idea of global peace seems no more than a beautiful dream, this meeting of the religious and spiritual leaders of the world brought a ray of hope to peace loving people everywhere.

The hearts of the participants were filled with love and enthusiasm, creating a reunion-like atmosphere among the members of the universal family. On the first day of the Summit, the programmes began with the blowing of the conch, Taiko drumming, and a deeply moving prayer session, creating a spiritually vibrant atmosphere such as the UN General Assembly had never before witnessed. The languages were different, but the deep and profound feelings were one and the same.

When Amma walked towards the stage on

the first day, the chief coordinator of the Summit, Mr. Bawa Jain, welcomed her, saying, "Most welcome Mother, will you bless us with your prayers?"

Amma has said: "Prayer means humility. Peace is an experience that fills all aspects of our life when we bow down to the whole of creation with humility." And now, in that same spirit, Amma offered two well-known Sanskrit prayers.

It is easy to utter words, but to clearly convey the meaning of what is being said in a way that will penetrate the deeper levels of consciousness is something that only a Self-realised soul like Amma can do. Her prayer created a very special atmosphere. Transmitting and awakening the sweet, soothing feelings of love and peace, her voice carried throughout the UN General Assembly hall like a cool gentle breeze.

Amma's speech the next day was delivered to a full house. Standing behind the podium that carried the emblem of the United Nations, Amma, the compassionate Mother of all, spoke in simple and lucid Malayalam.

There was much laughter when Amma told the story of the three spiritual leaders who decided to hold a meeting, and several times the delegates gave a standing ovation. They especially applauded her weapons reference: "Simply transferring the world's nuclear weapons to a museum will not in itself bring about world peace. The nuclear weapons of the mind must first be eliminated."

Amma's speech was unique in many ways. The substance was rich with the light of pure spiritual experience. Here, the voice of supreme peace, love and harmony was talking about the very qualities that she embodied, giving her message a special poignancy and meaning.

When Amma was interviewed by the BBC, PBS and other news media during the Summit, she emphasised the need for a forum of spiritual and religious leaders to discuss, formulate and implement spiritual solutions for the existing conflicts in society. She said, "The solutions already exist in the religious texts, as spiritual visions and insights. Our ancestors, the great saints and sages who attained the peak of human existence, have given us a lot of advice on how to lead a peaceful and harmonious life. The real question is whether we are willing to put that into practice."

There was a magical moment when a journalist

asked Mother what she would be if she could rule the world. Amma said, "I would be a sweeper." The journalist looked at her quizzically, and Amma explained with a laugh, "I would sweep everyone's mind clean!"

Dispelling the darkness that envelopes the human soul, bringing them out into the light of God's grace and beauty, Amma, the irresistible lover of the entire creation, prefers to describe herself as a humble sweeper of human minds, rather than as the world spiritual leader that she is.

It is beyond my capacity to describe Amma and the wisdom that she imparts to us. Awestruck as I always am, may I, in utter amazement, simply bow down before this incomprehensible phenomenon known as Amma.

—Swami Amritaswarupananda

# Introduction

Dag Hammarskjöld, the first General-Secretary of the United Nations, once said: "We have tried to make peace on this earth and we have failed miserably. Unless there is a spiritual renaissance, this world will know no peace." And now, at the beginning of the new millennium, the United Nations, for the first time in its fifty-five year history, had invited religious and spiritual leaders of different faiths from every region in the world to come together to forge an alliance with the United Nations. The goal of the Summit was to identify ways that the worldwide religious and spiritual communities could work together as interfaith allies with the United Nations on specific peace, poverty and environmental initiatives. The Summit was held from August 28 to 31, 2000, at the General Assembly Hall of the United Nations Headquarters and the Waldorf-Astoria Hotel.

August 28th was declared "Day of Prayer for World Peace." The Summit's Secretary-General, Bawa Jain, issued a statement: "We are asking people around the world, at any time of the day, to gather in their houses of worship, businesses, streets or homes to join the religious leaders as they enter the United Nations and gather in prayer for peace."

Some two thousand representatives of the world's spiritual and religious traditions attended this conference. Among these, thirty presented talks on the Summit's key issues. Officially, Mother was one of the voices for Hinduism, but her message was universal.

The first day was designed to gather the delegates and dignitaries together, to focus their attention upon the issues at hand, and to invoke the presence and blessings of the Divine upon the proceedings. After the delegates had taken their seats in the General Assembly Hall, Amma and the other presenters filed in silently, as in a walking meditation. They were seated, and the silence suddenly ended with the stunning reverberations of Taiko drumming. Somehow this juxtaposition of silence and powerful sounds seemed like a metaphor for this conference, in which people of different and often sharply contrasting persuasions, experiences and backgrounds had come together to nourish from this diversity a new and harmonious world community based on a shared commitment to peace. Mother would address exactly this matter the next day during her speech, when she would say:

*"The very words 'nation' and 'religion' tend to connote division and diversity. Each nation and faith has its own characteristics, ideologies and interests. This diversity may seem to create obstacles in fostering peace, happiness and prosperity in the world. Yet, in reality, it is this diversity that brings richness and beauty to the world and to human life—just as a bouquet made from a variety of flowers is more beautiful than a bouquet of flowers that are exactly the same."*

The same theme—unity in diversity—was echoed by Bawa Jain in his written welcome to the conference participants: "During our time together, we will be exploring how our religious and political institutions can work together to secure greater peace, restore the integrity of the environment and end the desperation of poverty." Religious and political institutions are not always comfortable partners; this conference called upon members of both to collaborate, trusting in their shared commitment to the betterment of humankind.

After the Taiko drumming and other opening ceremonies, Mr. Jain welcomed the assembled delegates, and then called upon the respected leaders of the world's religious and spiritual traditions to offer prayers. He called Amma with both the familiarity of a son and with utmost respect: "Mother, will you bless us with your prayers?"

Of course, in the literature Amma is listed as "Sri Sri Mata Amritanandamayi Devi, Hindu Spiritual Leader." But even on this grand occasion, the truth of her intimate relationship with the world could not be concealed. Speaking for the world, the General-Secretary of the Summit, who, like each one of us, is a child of the Divine, said, "Mother, will you bless us?"

This intimacy, which attends Amma wherever she goes—be it into the hut of a simple villager in Kerala, the home of the Prime Minister of India or the chambers of the United Nations—is invited by Amma's own bearing, her disarming simplicity, her graceful humility and unmistakable love towards everyone.

Amma chanted two prayers for the world, known to Hindus everywhere, two prayers chanted daily in all her ashrams, two prayers that epitomise the purposes of the Millennium Peace Summit. First Swami Amritaswarupananda translated them into English and then Mother chanted them in Sanskrit.

> *"Lead us from untruth to truth, from darkness to light, and from death to immortality.*
> *May all beings in all the worlds be happy.*
> *Om, peace, peace, peace."*

Those of us who were with Amma at the birth of this new millennium, at midnight on 31st December, 1999, in the Amritapuri temple, remember how she led the entire community in chanting that last prayer for nearly half an hour—and how, at the stroke of midnight, she went into samadhi. On New Year's Eve, she chanted in the intimacy of her ashram; but this time, she repeated the same prayer in the presence of the world's religious and spiritual leaders, in the chambers of the United Nations.

The second day of the conference included moments of prayer and music, but was primarily a day of speeches.

The Secretary-General of the United Nations, Kofi A. Annan, gave the Inaugural Address and later the Chair of the International Advisory Board for the conference, Dr. Maurice Strong, spoke on "Religion, Peace and the U.N." Next came the Keynote Address by Dr. Ted Turner,

Honorary Chair of the Summit, and Vice Chair of Time Warner Incorporated. Mr. Turner's informal style of talking captivated the audience, as he narrated in simple, straight-forward language the events that had helped him develop his own views of spiritual inclusiveness. It was clear from audience responses that his experiences struck a chord of recognition in many listeners, and that his basic attitude in support of religious dialogue and acceptance was shared.

It was during the session on "The Role of Religion in Conflict Transformation" that Amma delivered her speech; and for the first time in history the chambers of the United Nations General Assembly rang with the sound of the Malayalam language. Audience members using earphones were able to follow the speech, for Mother's words were simultaneously translated into English, French, Chinese and several other languages. The Assembly hall thundered with applause as Amma finished her speech.

For those not blessed with being in the General Assembly Hall on that auspicious day, this book is published, so that they may read for themselves what Mata Amritanandamayi communicated to the delegates at the Summit—and to the world.

When Amma returned to India a few days later, a large crowd and several news reporters welcomed her at the Cochin airport.

En route from the airport to Amritapuri, Amma was received by thousands of people as her car inched its way along the road full of well-wishers. In the local villages and along the seaside road to the Ashram, every household, irrespective of their religion or caste, honoured Amma in the traditional way—by lighting oil lamps in front of their homes, burning incense and waving camphor. Many offered garlands to Amma and showered her with flower petals. Enthusiastic cheers and firecrackers announced her progress. Amma spent four hours driving the last seven kilometres, taking time to give *prasad* [blessed offering] to everyone she passed. The enthusiasm and joy of the crowd reflected the pride they felt in that a *Mahatma* [great soul], who was one of their own, had presented the glory of their ancient culture before the world.

Om
asatoma sadgamaya
tamasoma jyotirgamaya
mrityorma amritamgamaya
Om shanti shanti shanti

*Lead us from untruth to truth*
*from darkness to light*
*from death to immortality*
*Om peace peace peace*

Om
lokah samastah sukhino bhavantu
lokah samastah sukhino bhavantu
lokah samastah sukhino bhavantu
Om shanti shanti shanti

*May all beings in all the worlds be happy*
*Om peace peace peace*

# LIVING IN HARMONY

*An Address Given by*
**Sri Mata Amritanandamayi Devi**
*at the Millennium World Peace Summit*
*of Religious and Spiritual Leaders*

*The United Nations General Assembly*
*August 29, 2000*

# Living in Harmony

*The Role of Religion in Conflict Transformation*

Salutations to everyone gathered here, who are verily the embodiments of love and the supreme Self.

We have stepped into the new millennium with great hopes and expectations of change. But though the numbers denoting the year are different, essentially nothing else has changed. The real change must happen within ourselves. For only when conflict and negativity are removed from within can we play a truly constructive role in establishing peace. With the goal of peace in mind, the invaluable efforts of the United Nations to bring nations together, thereby creating peace and harmony, merit much praise. Amma bows down in reverence before your inspiring, wholehearted efforts.

Countless millennia have gone by since the dawn of humanity. It has been a long journey in search of peace, prosperity and happiness. We have achieved remarkable progress. It is up to each one of us to make the new millennium richer and more fulfilling than previous ones. Our aim should be not just a flourishing and prosperous world, but a world distinguished by peace, co-operation, unity and compassion towards all living beings. There is also a need for the entire world to progress culturally, morally and spiritually.

Today there are hundreds of nations and faiths. The very words 'nation' and 'religion' tend to connote division and diversity. Each nation and faith has its own special characteristics, ideologies and interests. This diversity may seem to create obstacles in fostering peace, happiness and prosperity. Yet, in reality, it is this diversity that brings richness and beauty to the world and to human life—just as a bouquet made from a variety of flowers is more beautiful than a bouquet of flowers that are exactly the same.

No one can deny the diversity of the world, for this is its very nature. If we reach a deeper understanding and embrace the noblest human values in our lives, we will realise that the beauty of the world lies in this very diversity.

Through the ages, we have learned many lessons from a multitude of experiences, but we have failed in many areas as well. In the last century alone, we went through two world wars in which millions of men, women and children lost their lives. Recently, we have witnessed similar horrifying tragedies. The possibility of nuclear war continues to threaten the world. The spread of terrorism is a matter for global concern. Religious and ethnic persecution continues to plague humanity. Also of great concern are the growing problems of violence perpetrated by our youth, drug abuse, child abuse, and more. Countless people are dying each day of needless violence in our cities. Furthermore, the problems of starvation, poverty, disease, environmental pollution and the excessive exploitation of nature need to be dealt with in a practical way.

We are living in an era in which science and modern communication have brought the world together into one small community, reducing the barriers of time and space. Nowadays, a person can span the globe in the same time it previously took to travel within his or her home state or province. The latest developments in the field of telecommunications keep us informed instantaneously of events occurring in any part of the world. Events in one part of the globe affect the entire planet to a greater or lesser extent. But though the world has become closer through technology, we have not drawn closer in our hearts. In fact, people seem to be becoming more and more divided among themselves. For example, members of a family, though physically close, often live as if they are isolated islands. The knowledge and power we human beings have acquired have also made us more isolated and selfish, thereby sowing the seeds of conflict.

Societies and nations are comprised of individuals. If we look back through history, we can see that all conflicts originate from conflict within the individual. And what is the source of this inner conflict? It is the lack of awareness of our true nature, the one living power within us, of which we are all a part. The role of spirituality, true religion, is to awaken this awareness and to help us develop such qualities as love, empathy, tolerance, patience and humility.

There is one Truth that shines through all of creation. Rivers and mountains, plants and animals, the sun, the moon and the stars, you and I—all are expressions of this one Reality. Many who have realised this truth through their own experience have walked on this earth, and many are yet to come. Modern science is also edging its way towards the discovery of this same truth.

If world peace is to become a reality, peace and harmony first have to fill the heart of every individual. Love for humanity has to be awakened within us. Love and unity are not alien to human nature—they are our most fundamental instincts, the very foundation of our existence.

## The World is One Family

The world is one family, of which we are all members. Peace and unity prevail in a household when the individuals fulfil their duties and responsibilities with the awareness that each member is an integral part of the whole. Only when we work together as a global family, not merely belonging to a particular race, religion or nation, will peace and happiness once again prevail on this earth.

As I travel around the world, countless people come to me and share their sorrows. They are Hindus, Christians, Muslims—men and women of all religions and countries. Some have told me that a husband, wife or child has been killed in a religious clash. Sometimes the conflict is between Christians and Muslims, sometimes it is between Hindus and Muslims, and at other times between Christians and Hindus. Or it may be between some other religious groups or races or countries. At such times I am deeply pained. Conflicts like these arise because people do not go into the depth of their religion. They fail to imbibe the essential principles of their religion.

There were once two countries on either side of a lake. The people of these countries were traditionally enemies. One day there was a sudden storm and a few boats capsized. A man was swimming for his life when he saw another man drowning. He came to his aid and managed to save him. Having reached the shore, the two of them were so relieved that they embraced each other and started talking. Before long, they discovered that they belonged to the enemy countries and immediately hatred flared up in them. The one who had saved the other shouted, "Had I known you were my enemy, I would have left you to drown!" When this man didn't know the other's nationality, he was aware only of their common humanity; he felt an instinctive sense of brotherhood and compassion to such a degree that he risked his own life to save the other. For a moment, he was, above all, a human being, with the deepest, most decent human values; his other ties were of only secondary importance. We are all basically human beings, members of the same global family. Only thereafter do we become members of a religion or a country. Under no circumstances should our ties to a religion, society, or country make us forget our basic human values.

No one is an isolated island; we are all links in the great chain of life. With or without our knowledge, each action we perform has an effect on others. The vibrations of joy and sorrow, as well as the good and evil thoughts emanating from each living being, permeate this entire universe, influencing each one of us. This entire cosmos exists in a state of mutual dependence and support. Living in accordance with this principle of universal harmony is what is known as *dharma*. The sorrow of every living being in this world is our own sorrow, and the happiness of every living being is our own happiness. We cannot harm even a small ant without harming ourselves. In harming others, we harm ourselves. Similarly, when we help others, we are helping ourselves.

A man sits with a candle in front of his house at night. A sudden wind blows out the candlelight. It is only then that his eyes are opened to the beauty of the smiling full moon and the cool moonlight. No wind can extinguish the moonlight. Similarly, when we give up our selfishness, the bliss we receive in return is great and everlasting.

We should strive to reach a state in which we are able to view all beings of the world, both animate and inanimate, as a part of our own Self. Just as the right hand reaches out to aid the left hand when it is injured, the ability to feel the sufferings of all beings as our own, and an intense yearning to comfort them, should awaken within us.

Human beings have different natures and temperaments. Their ideas and desires are not always the same; they are often conflicting. But there is only one earth available for all of us to live on, so we have to resolve our conflicts right here. Today, we are capable of destroying this blue dot called earth that adorns the forehead of Mother Universe. But we also have the capacity to create heaven on earth. The future of humanity depends on the choice we make.

## Assimilating the Essence of Religions

The goal of all religions is one—purification of the human mind. To overcome our selfishness, to love and serve our fellow beings, to rise to the level of universal consciousness—these goals are common to all religions. The core of religion is to foster these human values and awaken the innate divinity in people.

Though the founders of all religions realised and practiced the noblest ideals in their lives, their followers have often failed to live up to those ideals. Instead of focusing on the essence of the religious principles of love and compassion, we focus on the external rituals and traditions, which vary from religion to religion. That is how these religions, which were originally meant to foster peace and a sense of unity among us, became instrumental in spreading war and conflict. If we are willing to abide by the essential principles of religions, without being overly concerned about their external features and superficial aspects, religion will become a pathway to world peace. This does not negate the importance of religious disciplines and traditions. Indeed, they have their own significance. They are necessary for our spiritual development. But we must remember that these traditions are the means to the goal, and not the goal itself.

Suppose a person has to cross a river by boat. Upon reaching the other shore, the traveller has to leave the boat and move onward. If he insists on clinging to the boat, his progress will be hampered. Similarly, we have to give more importance to the goal of religion and not be attached to the means. Religious leaders must stress the inner essence of religion and urge people to practice the ideals found there. This will help to resolve conflicts. We should remember that religion is meant for humanity, and not humanity for religion.

Many religious practices cater to the needs of

the times in which they came into being. While dealing with the problems of this modern age, we should be prepared to re-examine those practices and make changes in accordance with the times we are living in now. No religious leader or saint has ever said that love and tolerance are to be offered only to the believers in one's own religion. They are universal values. What the world needs today is not religious propaganda, but the focus on helping people to imbibe the essence of religion.

# A New Age of Harmony Among Religions

The measuring rod of a noble culture is its tolerance and broadness in accepting even divergent groups. It is in this light that we should approach today's problems and encompass all the different polarities. Let us overlook the slips and failures of the past. In this era of global cooperation, all religious groups should be ready to respond to the needs of the times. Relinquishing the outdated violent means, let us usher in a new era of fellowship and cooperation.

# Recognising Areas of Conflict

The world's religious leaders should participate in sincere, openhearted discussions, rooted in the understanding of the essential goals of religion. Through this we will reduce our misunderstandings and gain insight into major areas of conflict. To solve the complex and controversial issues of religious freedom, conversion, and fanaticism, religious leaders must come together in dialogue with open hearts in order to arrive at mutually acceptable, practical solutions.

However, for such discussions to be fruitful, we must first plant the seeds of love, peace and patience within ourselves. Only those who experience true peace within themselves can give peace to others. Until we rid ourselves of our own hatred and hostility, all our attempts to achieve everlasting peace are bound to fail; for our attempts will be tainted by our individual likes and dislikes.

The leaders of three religions—A, B and C—once decided to convene a meeting to bring about peace. God was so pleased with their efforts that He sent an angel to them during the meeting. The angel asked the leaders what they wished. The leader of religion A said, "Religion

B is responsible for all the problems. So please wipe them off the face of the earth!" The leader of religion B said, "Religion A is the cause of all our troubles. You have to reduce them to ashes!" By now the angel was disappointed. The angel turned expectantly to the leader of religion C. With an expression of grave humility, C's leader said, "I wish nothing for myself. It will be enough if you merely grant the prayers of my two colleagues!"

This story is a parody of contemporary efforts towards peace. Even as people smile at one another, hatred and distrust boil within. Peace is essential to all of us. Peace is not just the absence of war and conflict; it goes well beyond that: it is the spirit of harmony within ourselves. Peace should be fostered within the individual, within the family and within society. Simply transferring the world's nuclear weapons to a museum will not in itself bring about world peace. The nuclear weapons of the mind must first be eliminated. That is the role of religions.

# Cultivating Tolerance and Healing the Wounds of Conflict

A hallmark of civilisation is the open-mindedness to accept differing views and diverse people. We should be able to approach all problems with this attitude, and accept any differences that may arise. Forgetting the failures and shortcomings of the past, let today's religious leaders and representatives set a new example to the world through their broad-mindedness, mutual understanding and cooperation. What the world needs now more than anything else is living examples.

Religious leaders should take the lead in resolving religious conflicts and in re-establishing peace in their respective spheres of influence. These leaders should also come forth to play a constructive role in providing comfort and necessary aid to the victims of oppression.

In today's civilised, global society, religious interests should not be propagated by unfair means. The historic purpose of religion is not to build walls of division in society, but to knit people together with the thread of universal love.

# Freedom of Religion

Now is the time to welcome the birth of a new age of peace and friendship, rising above distrust and violence. The civilised world has accepted each person's right to follow and practice the faith of his or her choice. There are religious majorities and minorities all over the world. Spiritual leaders should encourage equal rights for all religions. We should strive to ensure that the basic rights of religious and ethnic minorities are safeguarded.

# The Problem of Conversion

The right to share the teachings of one's religion with others is generally accepted to be a part of religious freedom. However, conflict ensues when different religious groups compete with one another in spreading their religions and when they attempt to convert others. Today, many families and societies are falling apart because of such conflict. In response, the religious leaders should sit together and formulate guidelines acceptable to all faiths.

All the great religions have infinite wisdom and beauty to share. We should create opportunities for people everywhere, especially young people, to learn not only about their own religion, but also about other religions, and to become appreciative of their noble ideals. Instead of trying to increase the number of followers, religions should create an environment in which one may wisely accept the noble ideals of any religion. Let us go beyond religious conversion and work to eliminate narrow-mindedness and division. There is a mantra in the scriptures of *Sanatana Dharma*[1] that says, "May noble thoughts and ideals come to us from every where." Let this be the slogan of religions for the new millennium.

## Extremism

Fanaticism and the terrorism that it creates are two of the most serious problems facing the modern world. Religious extremism grows from poor understanding of the basic goals of religion, and from exploitation of religious sentiments. Religious leaders should discourage activities endangering human values, and should create a conscious movement against these deplorable actions.

---

[1] Popularly known as Hinduism

# Inner Transformation – The Key to Real Peace

The key to world peace lies with every individual residing on this planet. Just as each member of a household shares the responsibility of safeguarding the home, each of us shares the responsibility of world peace. Love and unity are not alien to human nature; they form the very foundation of human existence.

It is necessary to provide material needs such as food, clothing, shelter and health care, but this is not enough. We have to go much deeper. We have to attain abiding peace and happiness in our lives and in the world as a whole.

Religion is the science of the mind. It gives insight into the nature of the mind. Today we are able to air-condition the external world, but we have yet to learn how to air-condition the mind. We are trying to clone human beings, but we do not attempt to create within ourselves a perfect, loving and peaceful human being. An important part of religion is this purification process.

Today we are aware of the need to protect our environment, and this, of course, is essential. Yet we are seldom concerned with the pollution that negative thoughts and actions create in the atmosphere and in the consciousness of humanity. The inner pollution of the mind is in many ways more lethal than chemical pollution, for it has the power to destroy humanity at any time. We therefore need to purify our mental environment.

A lasting and positive transformation in society can be brought about only by correcting the human mind. After removing the impurities of egoism, jealousy, hatred and anger from within, religion lights the lamp of love in the hearts of humanity. The duty of religion is to inculcate virtues in the lives of the people, mould their character, and fill their minds with love and concern for their fellow beings.

## Spiritual Principles in Education

Tomorrow's world will be shaped by today's children. In their tender minds, it is easy to cultivate universal human values. If you walk through a field of soft, green grass a few times, you will quickly make a path; whereas it takes countless trips to forge a trail on a rocky hillside. The teaching of universal spiritual principles and human values should be a standard part of the general education, not only the responsibility of the family. This should not be delayed any further, for if there is delay, the future generations will be lost to the world.

Of great concern today are the countless youngsters who are feeling unloved, alienated and frustrated. They are being brought up in a society that teaches them to think, "What can I get?" rather than, "What can I give to the world?" They are being taught through the media that violence is a legitimate way to end any sort of conflict. Lacking the proper guidance and role models, many take to drugs as an escape from the challenges of life. This destroys their young minds; it is like a worm that is infesting a tender flower bud. Let us appeal to the media and educational institutions to participate in using their influence to transform the misdirected youth of today's society into kind, positive, peace-loving human beings.

## Economic Inequality

We cannot lose sight of the essential needs of people, for until these needs are met, it is impossible for anyone to aspire to higher states of awareness and understanding. If, in any part of the world, thousands of people are dying of hunger or suffering in poverty, it is a matter of shame for all nations. Based on the religious ideal of universal kinship, all nations and individuals that are in a position to do so should share their material wealth and resources. There is enough for the survival of all living beings on this earth, yet not enough to satisfy the greed of a few.

Religious leaders, along with individual nations, rulers and non-governmental organisations, should play a part in uplifting the downtrodden. Compassion towards our fellow beings is the first step in spirituality. God is not confined to any particular place, but is all-pervasive. God resides in all beings, both animate and inanimate. God should also be worshipped in the sick and poor. God's nature is pure compassion. Lending a helping hand to a neglected soul, feeding the hungry, giving a compassionate smile to the sad and dejected—this is the real language of religion. We should invoke God's compassion in our own hearts and hands. Only then will we experience deep joy and fulfilment in life. Living only for oneself is not life, but death.

## The Duty of Nations

This world is like a flower. Each nation is a petal of this flower. If one petal is infested, it will soon affect all the other petals, and the life and beauty of the flower will be destroyed. Realising this truth, the nations of the world should come forth and lay the foundation for a new golden era of cooperation and co-existence. Qualities such as love, sympathy and generosity are not meant only for individuals. They should become the very hallmark of each nation, and the soul of society.

We have risen from the dark ages when it was believed that war and colonisation were the duty of rulers. All nations and especially organisations such as the United Nations are coming forth to protect human rights and discourage oppression and dictatorship in all areas. Let the United Nations expand its activities into the higher realms of human consciousness. Harmony among nations will become possible only through the upliftment of individuals. With this in mind, the United Nations should encourage the spread of spiritual culture and the fostering of human values.

## No Effort is Futile

Some may say that the world will remain the same no matter how hard we try to change it. They may argue that striving for world peace is as useless as trying to straighten a dog's curly tail. However much we may try to straighten it, the tail will immediately curl back. Yet, through constant effort, we will build muscles even if the tail doesn't become straight. In the same way, regardless of whether we fail or succeed in bringing about world peace, we, ourselves, will change for the better. Even if there is no visible change, the change in us will eventually effect change in the world. Furthermore, whatever harmony exists in the world today is the result of such efforts.

It is pointless to brood over the past. The past is like a cancelled check—no longer valid. In order to create a positive future, given all the pain and destruction that have been inflicted in the past, we have to be willing to forgive; this is fundamental to all religions. Yet we must learn from the past, or we will repeat our mistakes. After a thorn pricks our foot, we become alert with each step; this alertness could be what saves us from falling into a dangerous pit further on. It is from this perspective that we should view the painful experiences of the past. Those who have harmed others in the past should now engage in positive actions to uplift the victims of their past oppression. These principles apply to governments as well as to individuals. Each nation should foster an atmosphere of forgiveness, openness, friendship, trust, help and support to heal old wounds. In order to heal the wounds, broken relationships should be stitched with the thread of love. For this to be possible, more than intellectual knowledge, we should have an awareness of our oneness.

The nations and religions that have fought with others in the past should come forward to create a new atmosphere of goodwill, trust and mutual support. Those nations that have invaded or exploited other nations and religions in the past should come forward to offer their assistance to the victimised nations. World peace is born out of mutual trust. If that trust is to grow, an atmosphere of friendship and cooperation is necessary.

Action is needed far more than words. A starving person's hunger will not be appeased if we just write on a paper, "The hungry should be fed." Let us focus on what we can give to others—not on what we can get for ourselves. Only then can we bring about a total transformation in our global family.

The following are some of the universally recognised problem areas in which the UN should strengthen their efforts:

ॐ In God's creation, men and women are equal. But over the centuries, the sad condition of women has not significantly improved. Women, who give birth to humankind, should be assured an equal role in society.

ॐ Millions of people are suffering from AIDS, and HIV continues to spread like wildfire. This disease must be brought under control.

ॐ The UN should strive to ensure religious freedom, encourage spiritual practices and spread human values, with the ultimate aim of creating broadminded individuals and resolving conflict.

ॐ Let the UN lead the transformation from a world of conflict to one of peace by training a group of youth to do community service. These young emissaries, serving selflessly throughout the world, will inspire people to cultivate universal and human values. What cannot be achieved through bloodshed can be achieved through love.

ॐ Terrorism and violence against human beings in the name of any religion should be condemned at the international level and appropriate strong action should be taken.

ॐ Excessive exploitation of Nature should be curtailed. We need to embrace an entirely new viewpoint and adopt a far-seeing policy that respects and considers the needs and aspirations of future generations. We may take what we need from Nature, but if we take with greed, our very existence will be endangered.

Material progress alone will not create peace or prosperity in the world. The need of the hour is progress that includes all areas of life. At the grassroots level, progress and expansion will result only from the love and the sense of duty towards our fellow beings that originate from a spiritual outlook. That progress and expansion should take place in the life of the individual and in society as a whole. The age we have just passed through was the Age of Science. Now it is time to bring in a new age—the Age of Love and Spirituality.

It is possible to realise the underlying unity of humanity while still being part of different religions, societies, races, cultures and nations—in fact, we are meant to do so. For if we integrate the most profound ideals of any religion into our own lives, we naturally become more expansive, and there awakens within us the awareness of the one, same Divine Reality that shines in all living beings. Selfishness will vanish, and our lives will thus become offerings to the world. In that state of selflessness, bliss will fill our hearts and overflow, reaching all beings.

In the end, love is the only medicine that can heal the wounds of the world. In this universe, it is love that binds everything together. Love is the very foundation, beauty and fulfilment of life. If we dive deep enough into ourselves, we will find that the one thread of universal love ties all beings together. As this awareness dawns within us, all disharmony will cease. Abiding peace alone will reign.

May the light of love and peace shine within our hearts. Let us all become messengers of universal peace, illuminating the hearts of everyone. Thus, let the glory of peace spread everywhere, dispelling the darkness of hatred and conflict that has overshadowed today's world. Let us all awaken to a new tomorrow, filled with universal love and kinship. This is the very goal and dream of the United Nations. May the *Paramatman*—the Supreme Power—shower grace upon us that we may realise this noble prayer.

# Book Catalog
## *By Author*

**Sri Mata Amritanandamayi Devi**
108 Quotes On Faith
108 Quotes On Love
Compassion, The Only Way To Peace: Paris Speech
Cultivating Strength And Vitality
Living In Harmony
May Peace And Happiness Prevail: Barcelona Speech
May Your Hearts Blossom: Chicago Speech
Practice Spiritual Values And Save The World: Delhi Speech
The Awakening Of Universal Motherhood: Geneva Speech
The Eternal Truth
The Infinite Potential Of Women: Jaipur Speech
Understanding And Collaboration Between Religions
Unity Is Peace: Interfaith Speech

**Swami Amritaswarupananda Puri**
Ammachi: A Biography
Awaken Children, Volumes 1-9
From Amma's Heart
Mother Of Sweet Bliss
The Color Of Rainbow

**Swami Jnanamritananda Puri**
Eternal Wisdom, Volumes 1-2

**Swami Paramatmananda Puri**
On The Road To Freedom Volumes 1-2
Talks, Volumes 1-6

**Swami Purnamritananda Puri**
Unforgettable Memories

**Swami Ramakrishnananda Puri**
Eye Of Wisdom
Racing Along The Razor's Edge
Secret Of Inner Peace
The Blessed Life
The Timeless Path
Ultimate Success

**Swamini Krishnamrita Prana**
Love Is The Answer
Sacred Journey
The Fragrance Of Pure Love
Torrential Love

**M.A. Center Publications**
1,000 Names Commentary
Archana Book (Large)
Archana Book (Small)
Being With Amma
Bhagavad Gita
Bhajanamritam, Volumes 1-6
Embracing The World
For My Children
Immortal Light
Lead Us To Purity
Lead Us To The Light
Man And Nature
My First Darshan
Puja: The Process Of Ritualistic Worship
Sri Lalitha Trishati Stotram

# Amma's Websites

**AMRITAPURI—Amma's Home Page**
*Teachings, Activities, Ashram Life, eServices, Yatra, Blogs and News*
http://www.amritapuri.org

**AMMA (Mata Amritanandamayi)**
*About Amma, Meeting Amma, Global Charities, Groups and Activities and Teachings*
http://www.amma.org

**EMBRACING THE WORLD®**
*Basic Needs, Emergencies, Environment, Research and News*
http://www.embracingtheworld.org

**AMRITA UNIVERSITY**
*About, Admissions, Campuses, Academics, Research, Global and News*
http://www.amrita.edu

**THE AMMA SHOP—Embracing the World® Books & Gifts Shop**
*Blog, Books, Complete Body, Home & Gifts, Jewelry, Music and Worship*
http://www.theammashop.org

**IAM—Integrated Amrita Meditation Technique®**
*Meditation Taught Free of Charge to the Public, Students, Prisoners and Military*
http://www.amma.org/groups/north-america/projects/iam-meditation-classes

**AMRITA PUJA**
*Types and Benefits of Pujas, Brahmasthanam Temple, Astrology Readings, Ordering Pujas*
http://www.amritapuja.org

**GREENFRIENDS**
*Growing Plants, Building Sustainable Environments, Education and Community Building*
http://www.amma.org/groups/north-america/projects/green-friends

**FACEBOOK**
*This is the Official Facebook Page to Connect with Amma*
https://www.facebook.com/MataAmritanandamayi

**DONATION PAGE**
*Please Help Support Amma's Charities Here:*
http://www.amma.org/donations

www.ingramcontent.com/pod-product-compliance
Lightning Source LLC
Chambersburg PA
CBHW061346040426
42444CB00011B/3107